Bullet Journal

For Beginners

Bullet Journal Notebook Planner With Grid Layouts

What is a Bullet Journaling?

Bullet journaling is an easy way for you to track your past activity, plan your present activity and prepare for future events and activities. The system is growing in popularity on a daily basis as it is the perfect way to track your progress against the tasks and goals that you make in your life. It is a great way to keep a more visual record of your day to day life, work, health or business. The bullet journaling system also enables you to take a reflective look at your progress to see how far you have come in relation to the goals that you set for yourself.

The first thing to remember about Bullet Journaling is that **there is no set system or layout to suit everyone**. The system has a familiar structure which is built around an **Index Page**, a **Future Log**, A **Monthly Log** and a **Diary Log**.

This is your own personal bullet journal for you to design as you like. There is a blank page and also a dotted page which can both be used to design and journal as you like. You cannot make mistakes in it because it is yours and yours alone. We suggest you try different grid layouts and adapt them to suit you. You may want to incorporate daily, weekly, monthly or annual layouts in your bullet journal or include a variety of other pages too, just don't get bogged down with the design, it is intended to aid productivity, not paralyze you into thinking about the 'best' layout for hours, days or even weeks!

What Layouts Should I Use?

Included at the back of the book are some common grid layouts that you can copy yourself by simply getting a pencil and a ruler and making some lines. All these layouts are proven to aid productivity and improve your workflow. It is best to design your layouts in pencil first, that way you can simply rub any mistakes out and start over. Once you are satisfied with the design of your pages you can go over the pencil lines with a more permanent marker if you like.

Use lots of color, doodles, sticky Post It tabs and flags to separate and define your pages, especially the ones that you need to use on a daily basis. Bullet Journals look great when you use washi tape to divide the journal into sections. With a little bit of creativity and you can give your bullet journal your own unique style. Remember, you cannot go wrong in laying out the pages in your Bullet Journal, each page will be designed by you and will be personal to your own unique style.

The Bullet Journal Key System

Some of the most common symbols used in the Bullet Journal system are illustrated below.

Bullet Journal Key System

The Bullet key system helps you to organize your daily entries by giving you the opportunity to do a complete 'brain dump' by writing absolutely everything down. Each time you list an entry or write anything in your journal use the key symbols throughout to stay consistent in your journaling and goal-setting activities.

Journaling this way gives each task, goal, habit, routine or activity that you list some life as well as giving you a quick visual overview on the progress of your goals, tasks and actions so that you know what you have accomplished, what you are focusing on now and what you need to record and execute in the future

Organizing your Bullet Journal on a Daily Basis

The first thing you need to do is to number the first ten pages. It should then be organized using the following key pages:

1. Index
2. Future Log
3. Monthly Log
4. **Daily Log**
5. **Customized Bullet Journal Grid Pages**

The **Index** page is the place you list all the pages and / or topics as you write them in your journal. Much like a table of contents, it is designed to help you find your entries easily. It can be as simple as the illustration below:

Index	
Topic	**Page**
Future Log	2
My 2017 Goals	3 - 4
March Monthly Log	5 - 6
Books To Read	7
Quotes I Like	8
Exercise / Fitness Tracker	9 - 10

The Future Log Page

The Future Log is the place for you to schedule things for the future or list the things that you want to get around to if you have time.

Any goal/task that you have not managed to achieve in this period can simply be re-scheduled to your next Future Log.

This page is designed to help you find your entries easily. Put a date next to important items to remind you when they are taking place. The page can be designed as simply as shown in the illustration below. Using a two-page spread to cover a six-month period works well and it also looks good.

FUTURE LOG

Jan
- 4 - Renew gym membership
- 7 - Start Fields Campaign
- 19 - Presentation (Harris)

Feb
- 22 - Attend WT Conference
- 28 - Start media course outline

Mar
- 8 - Martha's birthday
- 30 - Birch Agency Design Brief

Apr
- Plan Annual WT Summit
- 11 - Camp

May
- 13 - Outdoor Adventure Trail
- Start house renovation

Jun
- Plan Vacation / Caribbean

The Monthly Log

The Monthly Log page is self-explanatory and is used to list all the tasks that you have for the month. On the left hand page list the days of the month and on the right hand page list all your tasks.

This page is used as a bit of a brain dump and also serves as a quick reference for jotting down everything that you have to do. It is a good idea to leave a bit of space on the left hand side of the calendar page so you can add icons from the Key System next to your entries.

The Daily Log

This page is used to list your tasks and events for the day as well as a placeholder for taking quick notes. On this page you should use the symbols from the **Key System** to identify the status of all your entries.

Just fill it out day by day using additional pages if you need to. Don't forget to migrate tasks where applicable. The picture below illustrates how you can design your daily log. Some people like to fill this section out first thing then track the tasks throughout the day.

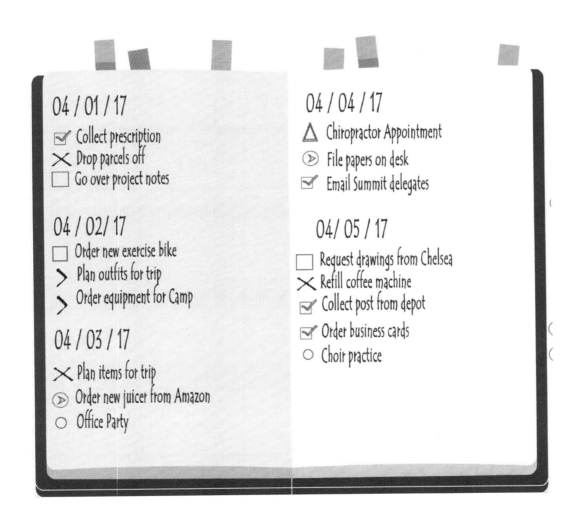

YOUR BULLET JOURNAL
STARTS HERE

You have 2 styles of pages
Blank pages and Dot Bullet pages

Bullet List Layout Page Examples

As well as using the five key pages in your bullet journal, a lot of people like to use different layouts to record and track different things. Because we are all different, what works for one person may not work for someone else. Each person's journal is personal to them and there are a therefore a variety of layouts that you can use to satisfy your bulleting desires. Included at the back of this book are some great ideas for layouts that you can create, customize and tweak until you are happy with a page that serves your needs.

As well as a comprehensive list of Bullet Journal page layout ideas, you will find plenty of layouts that have been specially designed to give you a good idea of the different ways that you can record your information. Used correctly, they are very effective at organizing your life. They are different in size and font and some have room on the page so you can add sticky notes, drawings and doodles in the blank areas.

Use these pages when designing your own pages on the blank sheets included throughout this journal. All you need is a pencil and ruler and you can start designing your own unique pages. All the designs are simple and easy to replicate.

Example Layouts / Pages Included:

- Monthly Goals Planner
- Double Spread Weekly Planner
- Double Spread Weekly Workout / Food Journal
- Gratitude Journal
- Goals Sheet
- Daily Scheduler
- Weekly Planner
- Custom One Page Productivity Planner
- Grid Layout
- Dot Layout
- Recipe Journal
- Password Log
- Weekly Meal Planner Sheet
- Trip / Day Out Memory Journal
- Dream Journal
- Birthdays List
- Prayers and Notes Journal
- Things That Make Me Happy Journal

Content Dividers

You can use a variety of dividers in your content to give your journal a more customized and visually pleasing look and in order to make each section distinct from the others. There is a set of hand drawn dividers below which will give you a good idea of some of the styles you can use. This makes your bullet journal unique to you.

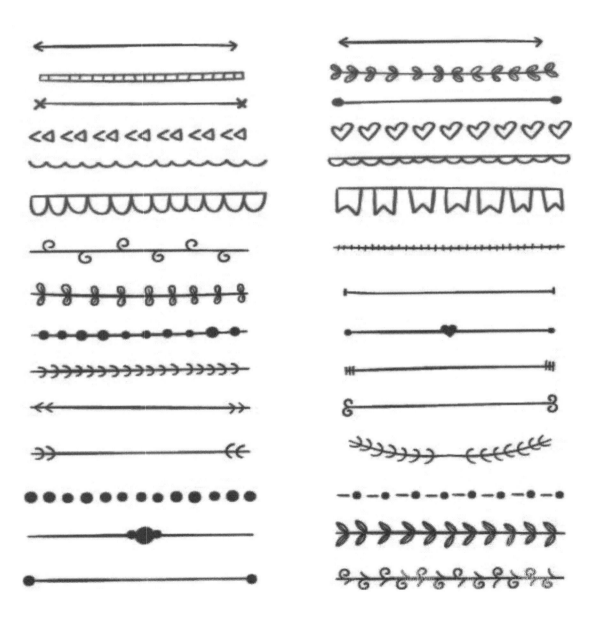

Other Great Ideas For Your Bullet Journal Page Layouts

PRODUCTIVITY PAGES

- Daily Goals
- Weekly Goals
- Monthly Goals
- Goal Tracker
- Priorities Tracker
- Mind Maps

TO DO PAGES

- Daily "To-Do" List
- Bucket List
- Movies to See
- Movies to Watch
- TV Shows to Watch / Episode Tracker
- Restaurants to Try
- Books to Read
- Places to Visit / Travel

PLANNING PAGES

- Weekly Calendar
- Monthly Calendar
- Yearly Calendar
- Family Schedule
- Brainstorming Ideas Page
- DIY / Home Renovation Projects
- Shopping / Grocery List
- Budget / Finance Planner
- Hobbies List

IMPORTANT DATES PAGES

- Birthday Planner
- Holiday / Vacation Planner
- Special Event Dates
-

HEALTH / FITNESS PAGES

- Meal Planning
- Favorite Recipes
- New Recipes to Try
- Migraine Tracker
- Sleep Tracker
- Food Tracker
- Exercise Plan / Workout Routines
- Water Tracker

BLOGGING / WORK PAGES

- Editorial Calendar
- Blog Post Ideas
- Income / Expenses
- Social Media Tracking
- Blog Deadlines/Schedule
- Hashtags Page
- Meetings Notes / Minutes
- Courses to Take / Complete
- Products to Create
- Videos to Make

MORE PAGE IDEAS

- Ideas Page
- Quotes to Remember
- Favorite Poems / Lyrics
- Thought for the Day
- New Accomplishments
- Things to Learn
- Wish lists
- Challenges (i.e. 7, 14 or 21 Day Challenge)
- Gratitude Journal Page
- Sketches / Artwork / Doodle Page

The following section contains the Bullet Journal example layouts.

Fun

☐ _____
☐ _____
☐ _____
☐ _____
☐ _____

Self Improvement

☐ _____
☐ _____
☐ _____
☐ _____
☐ _____

Family & Friends

☐ _____
☐ _____
☐ _____
☐ _____
☐ _____

Health

☐ _____
☐ _____
☐ _____
☐ _____
☐ _____

Monthly Goals

Financial

☐ _____
☐ _____
☐ _____
☐ _____
☐ _____

Work

☐ _____
☐ _____
☐ _____
☐ _____
☐ _____
☐ _____
☐ _____
☐ _____
☐ _____
☐ _____
☐ _____

Home

☐ _____
☐ _____
☐ _____
☐ _____
☐ _____
☐ _____

Other Goals

☐ _____
☐ _____
☐ _____
☐ _____
☐ _____
☐ _____
☐ _____
☐ _____

Mon	**Tue**	**Wed**

Daily Tracker

	M	T	W	T	F	S	S

Meal Planner

M	
T	
W	
T	
F	
S	
S	

- ☐ _____
- ☐ _____
- ☐ _____
- ☐ _____
- ☐ _____

Thu	**Fri**	**Sat**

Tasks	**Notes**	**Sun**

Tasks

- ☐ _____
- ☐ _____
- ☐ _____
- ☐ _____
- ☐ _____
- ☐ _____
- ☐ _____

WEEKLY WORKOUT / FITNESS JOURNAL

Date	Exercise / Activity	Sets	Reps	Notes / Summary

Summary of my week

Weight

Food Journal

DATE	Breakfast	Lunch	Dinner	Snacks	Total
Mon					
Calories					
Tue					
Calories					
Wed					
Calories					
Thu					
Calories					
Fri					
Calories					
Sat					
Calories					
Sun					
Calories					

<u>*Summary of my week*</u>

Day _____   Date _____

Today I am **Grateful** for:

----

*"Do not spoil what you have by desiring what you
have not; remember that what you now
have was once among the things
you only hoped for."— Epicurus*

Day _____   Date _____

Today I am **Grateful** for:

GOAL

DATE

STEPS | DONE

1

2

3

4

GOAL

DATE

STEPS | DONE

1

2

3

4

GOAL

DATE

STEPS | DONE

1

2

3

4

Date: _____

Schedule:

To Do List

Future Tasks

Gratitude List

Notes

| DATE | .... |

MONDAY

TUESDAY

WEDNESDAY

THURSDAY

FRIDAY

SATURDAY

SUNDAY

DATE:

TODAY'S TOP 3 GOALS	Done? Y/N
1.	
2.	
3.	

TO DO's	Done? Y/N

Phone Calls & Emails ☎

Chores

To Buy / Shopping List

APPOINTMENTS / MEETINGS

Time	Who / Where

NOTES

Productivity Score For Today | /10

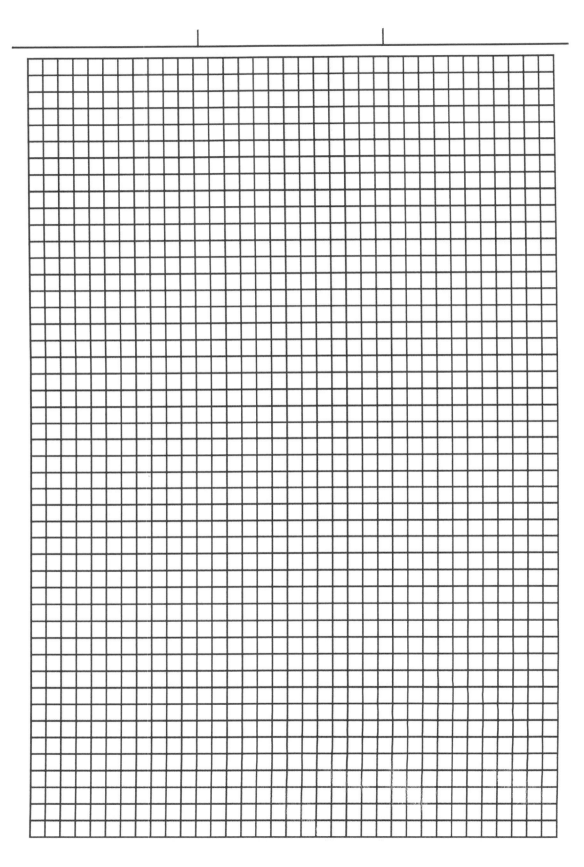

Recipe Name			
Serves	Prep Time	Cooking Time	Oven Temp

Ingredients

Directions

Notes

Website:	
User Name:	
Password:	
Associated email:	
Notes:	

Website:	
User Name:	
Password:	
Associated email:	
Notes:	

Website:	
User Name:	
Password:	
Associated email:	
Notes:	

Website:	
User Name:	
Password:	
Associated email:	
Notes:	

	Week of:			Budget:
	Breakfast	**Lunch**	**Dinner**	**To Buy**
Mon				
Tue				
Wed				
Thu				**Notes**
Fri				
Sat				
Sun				

Date of my Trip: ____/____/____ *Place:* _____

Memories of the Day
Write about what you did the best part of the day, who or what you saw or anything else interesting about your trip.

Day: _____   **Date:** _____

Dream Description:

_____

_____

_____

_____

_____

_____

_____

The Type of Dream:

Nightmare   Fantasy   Symbolic   Exciting   Boring   Crazy

Dream Interpretation (What I think it meant):

_____

_____

_____

_____

Emotion Tracker (What / How my dream made me feel):

Anger	☐	Happy	☐	Peace	☐
Fear	☐	Freedom	☐	Love	☐
Shame	☐	Joyful	☐	Confused	☐
Sad	☐	Surprised	☐	Other: _____	

Is This a Recurring Dream?   Yes ☐   No ☐

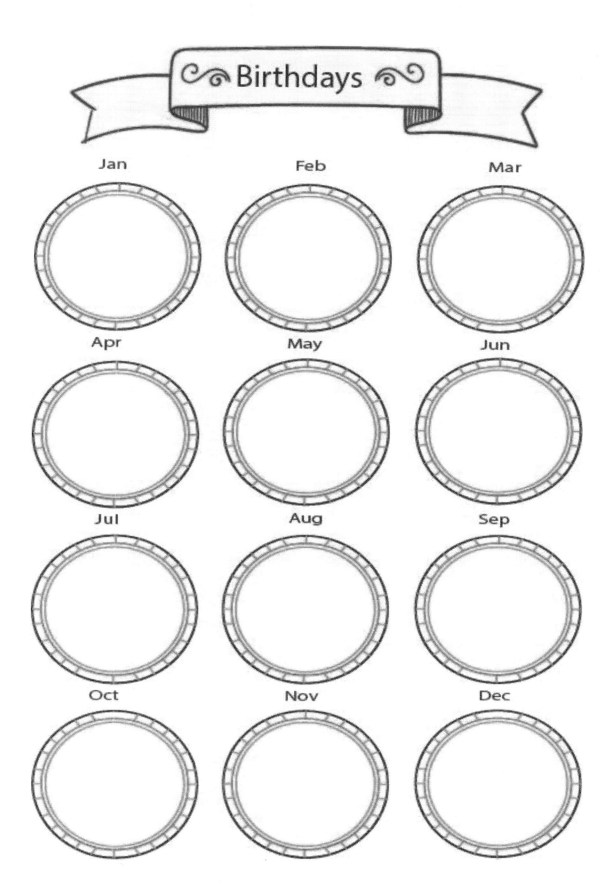

Prayers & Notes

Date: / /

Today's Scripture

Book: _____

Chapter: _____ Verse: _____

People To
Pray For

_____
_____
_____
_____
_____
_____

How did the Lord speak to me in this scripture:

_____
_____
_____
_____
_____
_____

Affirmation / Lord help me to...

_____
_____
_____
_____
_____

Notes:

_____
_____
_____
_____
_____
_____

Things That Make Me Happy

Important Notes

Need Another Bullet Journal?
Visit **www.blankbooksnjournals.com**

Made in the USA
San Bernardino, CA
03 December 2017